HOW TO...
Ballet

A step-by-step guide to the secrets of ballet

Written by Jane Hackett

LONDON, NEW YORK, MUNICH,
MELBOURNE, and DELHI

Senior editor Carrie Love
Senior art editor Rachael Foster
Designer Lauren Rosier
US editor Margaret Parrish

Photographer Ruth Jenkinson
Production editor Siu Chan
Production controller Claire Pearson
Publishing manager Bridget Giles
Art director Martin Wilson
Creative director Jane Bull
Category publisher Mary Ling

First published in the United States in 2011 by
DK Publishing
375 Hudson Street, New York, New York 10014

Copyright © 2011 Dorling Kindersley Limited

11 12 13 14 15 10 9 8 7 6 5 4 3 2 1
179456–05/11

A catalog record for this book
is available from the Library of Congress.

ISBN: 978-0-7566-7580-6

Printed and bound in China
by Toppan

**Discover more at
www.dk.com**

Contents

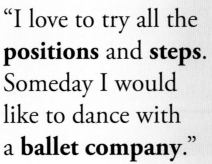

"I love to try all the **positions** and **steps**. Someday I would like to dance with a **ballet company**."

Introduction

You can dance anywhere and any way, and there are many different kinds of dancing. This book is about ballet, a beautiful form of dancing that has existed for many years. Ballet is elegant and graceful, but it is also lively and exciting.

This book tells you what you will need if you go to ballet classes, and it shows you the basic ballet positions and explains more difficult steps. As you follow the pages, you will learn how to join steps to make dances, and how to prepare for a performance. It also gives you a look into life at ballet school, and a ballet company.

Ballet is not easy, and some things take a lot of practise, so don't worry if you can't do everything at first. Keep practising and the steps will get easier—it's such a great feeling to learn something new, especially when you can perform for your family and friends.

Jane Hackett

Learning ballet is fun because it includes so many things—you will learn about your body, about music, performance, and theater. You can work with friends to make group dances or, when you are confident, you can dance solo dances. There is always something new to learn as you get older, stronger, and more confident.

"Dancers never stop learning. There is always something new to practise."

In pas de deux, two dancers can show beautiful lines and balances.

Why do so many steps have *French* names?

Pas de chat
(Pah-de-sha)

Sauté
(Soh-tay)

Échappé
(Ay-shap-ay)

"Cat step"

"Jump"

"To escape"

Ballet began in France more than three hundred years ago. It was danced in the court of King Louis XIV, the Sun King. Dancers turned their legs out to show their elegant feet and ankles—this is how "turnout" in ballet started. Ballet dancers all over the world use the same French names for steps and positions.

Before you start

There are some simple things you can do to get ready for your ballet class. The right clothes, shoes, and hairstyle will help you to move freely, and some simple exercises will warm your muscles and get your body ready to dance.

It's good to know the basic positions in ballet and learn the names of some of the steps and positions. Most ballet terms have French names because ballet started in France. At the back of this book you will find a glossary that will help you learn the words used in ballet.

Getting ready

It's important to have the right clothes and shoes for classes. Your clothes should fit your body well so that they don't get in the way when you move. This also allows your teacher to check your posture.

For the girls
Girls usually wear a leotard, short socks, and ballet shoes until they get older and then they wear tights. Some dancers add a skirt or belt.

See how to make a bun hairstyle on page 51.

If it is cold, wear a crossover cardigan until you have warmed up.

Tuck your tights over a belt to make sure that they are neat at the waist.

For the boys
Boys wear a close-fitting, stretchy T-shirt, shorts, and ballet shoes. Older boys wear a T-shirt or leotard with tights over the top and light-colored socks.

Always check with your teacher before buying shoes and a uniform.

Boys and girls wear light-colored socks and shoes so their ankles and feet can be seen clearly.

Adjustable drawstring

Soft sole

TYPES OF SHOE

There are quite a few kinds of ballet shoe. For class, shoes are usually canvas or leather because they last longer and can be cleaned. Shiny satin shoes are usually used for performances. You will need to sew elastic on your shoes to keep them in place when you dance.

BUYING SHOES

There are important things to remember when buying shoes:
1. The soles must be soft enough to bend with your foot and should not slip on the floor.
2. They must be carefully fitted to your feet: close enough to show the shape of your foot but not so tight that your toes curl up.

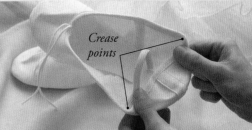

How to sew elastic on your shoes:

Crease points

1. Bend the back of your shoe forward

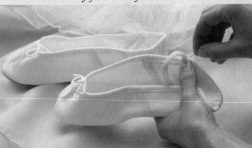

2. Sew the elastic at the crease points on the side.

1

2

3

Braided hairstyle

1. Make a center parting and two high bunches before braiding.

2. Pin one braid securely in place before doing the same with the other one.

3. Add a hair net and ribbons. Make sure they will not come loose as you spin.

Warming up

It's important to get your body warm and ready to dance. Warming up before you start your exercises will ensure that your muscles and joints are safe and you can make the most of your class.

Warm up gently before you begin to stretch.

To start with...

When you exercise, your heart beats faster and pumps more blood around your body. This warms your muscles so that you can stretch. Remember to be gentle when you are warming up and repeat each exercise several times.

Fingers and hands

1. Close your hands into tight fists, then stretch your fingers out wide.

2. Close your fingers in, one by one, then open them out in reverse order.

3. Pretend you are tapping your fingers on a window in front of you.

Neck

This should be done gently and slowly. Try to keep your shoulders soft and still.

1. Drop your ear toward your shoulder, looking straight forward. Repeat slowly to the other side.

2. Turn your head from left to right, looking toward the direction your head is turning.

Stretching exercises

The exercise that Beverley is showing will warm and stretch different parts of her body—her back and shoulders, her feet, ankles, and legs, especially the big muscles that go up the back of the legs and into the hips. These are what we call *hamstrings*.

1. **Sit on the floor** with your legs stretched in front and your back straight, arms stretched over your head.
2. **Start stretching** forward from the bottom of your back. Your head is the last part to come over your body. Relax your arms and stay there for 10 counts.
3. **Slowly curl** your back up until you are sitting straight again.

Stretch forward from the bottom of your back.

Hamstring stretch

2.

Shoulders and neck relaxed

Back straight

Stomach gently pulled in

Toes and insteps fully stretched

Soft stretch behind knees at first

1.

Back and neck straight

Shoulders relaxed

Hip joints warming up and opening

Hands lightly resting on ankles

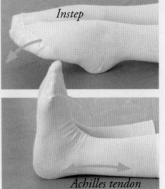

Instep

Achilles tendon

Foot and ankle stretch

A correct foot position is not just stretching your toes; it starts from above your ankle. Do this slowly, counting to three for each movement:

1. **Stretch** your ankle, the top of your foot (the instep) and finally your toes.
2. **Reverse** the movement, pulling your toes as far back toward you as you can, feeling the stretch behind your ankle (Achilles tendon).

Hip stretch

All the positions and steps in ballet are danced with the legs turned outward. This turnout must start from the hip joint at the top of your leg. Many of the exercises that you will learn are to help make your hips flexible and strong. This is a good stretch to put in your warm-up, and then to repeat at the end of class.

Knees sretching outward toward floor

Good posture

One of the first things you will learn is how to stand correctly; this is called good posture. When you are standing tall, with your arms and legs placed in the right way, you will find it easier to make ballet positions.

Keep your eyes forward; don't look down.

Imagine a line across your shoulders and across your hips.

Stomach muscles gently pulled in.

In bras bas, hands are held away from your legs.

Stand tall

With your feet firmly placed on the ground, you can feel the strength in your leg muscles and stomach. Then your shoulders and neck can relax with your arms in a gentle curved *bras bas*. Hold your head high like Beverley, and look straight ahead.

Shoulders relaxed down, keeping them wide and flat behind.

Legs evenly turned out from the hips.

Thigh muscles together

Calves together

Heels together

Check your posture in the mirror.

Symmetry

Both sides of your body should be the same. Feel that you have the same body weight on both feet with all your toes on the ground. It is easier to practice this when you are standing still or moving slowly.

Imagine a straight line running from your heels, up your legs and spine, to the top of your head.

Think of standing on triangles under your foot.

Weight evenly on both feet.

Looking forward

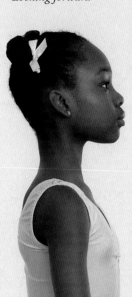

More posture tips

Try to feel that your shoulders, hips, knees, and feet are in a straight line underneath each other. Imagine that the end of your spine points down between your heels, but don't be stiff. Your spine should be flexible, ready to move smoothly.

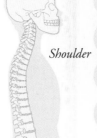

Shoulder

Hip

Knee

Your spine will have a small curve in it. Heels, hips, and shoulders are in line.

Your stomach muscles are your core, or center.

Ankle

All ballet positions require turnout

From the simplest posture standing still to the most difficult steps, you should keep your legs turned out. As your muscles learn to do this, you will be able to hold your turnout even when you jump and move fast.

Turnout of the legs starts at the hips

The hip joints gently turn outward and the legs follow. Don't try and turn your feet out too far, or you will hurt your knees. Start with a small V shape and, with practice, your legs will turn out more.

TURNOUT

Turnout when learning

Ideal turnout

Feel your whole foot stretch

Each time you do a *tendu*, or stretch, of your foot, begin the stretch in your ankle, then instep, and finally your toes as you slide your foot away from you. Use the muscles under your foot to push your toes along the floor.

What's where in your foot

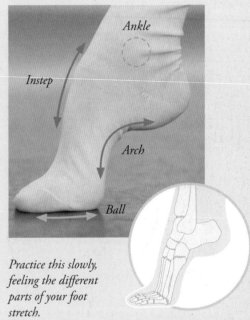

Ankle

Instep

Arch

Ball

Practice this slowly, feeling the different parts of your foot stretch.

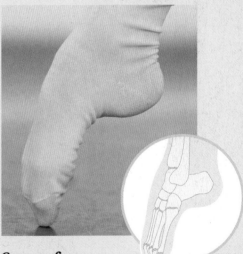

Strong feet

will help you balance, rise onto *demi-pointe*, jump in the air, and land safely. Dancers like to have arched feet because they continue the lines and shapes that the legs make. When you dance *en pointe* (on the tips of your toes), your feet are stretched like this inside your shoe.

Shoulders and neck relaxed

Stomach gently pulled in

1

First position

This is your starting position.

Arms: Lift your arms into a circle in front of you.

Legs: Standing straight, with good posture, turn your legs out from your hips until your feet are in a V shape.

Heels together

Basic positions

There are five basic positions of the arms and legs in ballet. All ballet positions and steps move through these positions. They seem simple at first, but you will find that there are lots of things to think about to make them as perfect as you can.

The five basic ballet positions

Once you can easily do the basic positions, you will start to learn the more difficult ones. There is a range of different ways the positions can be joined together and danced.

Remember, you will need good posture to make correct positions. There is an arm and leg position for each number. When you start ballet, like Hannah, you will only use first, second, and third positions. As you progress, you will learn fourth and fifth positions.

Practice first, second, and third

Correct feet positions

As you move from first to second then third position, keep your legs turned out and your feet pointing outward in the V shape. In all the positions, your weight should be evenly on both feet.

Try to keep your ankles strong and all five toes on the floor, so your feet don't raoll forward.

Hands lower than shoulders

Curved first position for one arm

The other arm remains stretched out to the side, as in second position.

2

Second position

Arms: Keep your arms in a curved shape as you open them to the sides. Your hands should be lower than your shoulders.

Legs: Holding the same turn out of your legs as in first position, move your feet apart. Not too wide— your heels should be under your hips and your weight evenly on both feet.

Weight evenly between both feet

Heels under hips

3

Third position

Arms: The arm above your front foot closes back into the round shape of first position.

Legs: Keeping your legs turned out, place one leg slightly in front of the other. Legs close together and the heel of your front foot is touching the side of your back foot, halfway along.

positions before starting to learn the fourth and fifth.

More positions

Fourth and fifth position are more difficult than first to third, since they require flexibility in the hip joints to give stronger turnout of the legs.

Your hands should be above your head with the width of your face between them.

Take one arm out to the side, as in second position.

Fourth open (ouvert)

Don't forget to take your body weight forward so your hips are evenly between your feet.

Fourth crossed (croissée)

4

Fourth position

Start with arms and legs in first position.

Arms: Lift the arm over your front foot into a round position above your head.

Legs: Slide one foot forward in front of you, keeping legs turned outward. The space between your feet should be equal to the length of your foot.

Start in third or fifth position so that your feet are one in front of the other when you slide forward.

Hold your turnout

5

Fifth position

Arms: Both arms are lifted up in a round position.

Legs: This is nearly the same leg position as third, but it requires greater turnout from the hips as the front foot crosses farther across the back foot. The leg muscles pull tightly toward each other and the knees are straight.

Difference between fifth and third feet positions

Don't worry if it takes you longer to learn fourth and fifth.

Port de bras in French means *"carrying (using) the arms"*.

Demi-bras *"half arms"*

The arms are halfway between first and second, hands turned up.

Bras bas *"arms low"*

This low curved shape will be the starting position for everything. Keep your hands clear of your skirt.

Demi-seconde *"half second"*

Arms are halfway between second and *bras bas*.

Fifth position of the arms is an elegant, beautiful position. Your arms should be like a picture frame for your face.

Fingers are soft and continue the curved shape of the position.

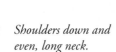

Shoulders down and even, long neck.

Another position

Boys will sometimes use this position. One arm is in *demi-bras* and the other hand is on the hip. Girls might use this arm position in a character or national dance.

At the *barre*

A ballet class usually starts with exercises at the *barre*. A *barre* is a long handrail that you hold on to lightly to help you keep your balance. Then you can concentrate on doing the moves as perfectly as you can.

You will start at the *barre* with slow bends and stretches, keeping the feet close to the ground. As you follow each sequence, your legs will lift higher and your movements will be bigger or quicker. Every exercise is designed to stretch a different part of your body and to make it stronger.

Perfect *pliés*

Plié is a French word that means "to bend." You will practice *pliés* in every class to make your leg muscles warm and strong. *Pliés* can be done in any of the five positions.

Shoulders even and relaxed.

Lightly rest your hands on the barre.

Demi-plié is a half bend

Grand plié is a full bend

Stomach gently pulled in.

Hips level

Thigh muscles open out from the hip.

Knees open over your feet.

Your plié is like a spring—it gives you the power to jump in the air. You cannot jump or relevé from straight legs. You must plié first.

Ankles strong

You will learn *pliés* facing the *barre*. Holding the *barre* helps to keep your shoulders and hips level while you concentrate on bending and stretching in the correct position. You will only do *demi-pliés* until your legs are strong enough to do a full *plié*.

Heels together and toes flat on the floor.

Demi-plié in first position

Plié in first

Just practise *demi-pliés* at first. When you have a good smooth movement, follow the whole sequence to go down into a grand *plié* and reverse it to come up. Don't pull yourself up on the *barre*— your leg and stomach muscles should lift you back up.

1. Stand with heels together in first position. Your legs should be turned out from the hips, hands lightly on the *barre*.

2. *Demi-plié* Keep your heels on the floor as you bend, pushing your thighs and knees out to make a diamond shape.

3. *Grand plié* As you go lower, your heels will lift up. As you go back up, push your heels on the floor and keep your back straight.

Plié in second

Stand evenly on both feet. Try to keep hips and shoulders level as you go up and down smoothly. Look forward and don't be tempted to look down. Don't go too low in any of the *grand pliés*—your bottom should not be below your knees.

1. Your heels are under your hips. Keep all your toes on the floor so that your ankles are not rolling forward.

2. *Demi-plié* Keep your legs turned out from the hips on the way down and up. This will strengthen your turnout.

3. *Grand plié* When you reach the *grand plié*, try to have your knees out and thighs in a straight line before going back up.

Third position

When you have learned all your *plié* positions facing the *barre*, you can begin to practice them with one hand holding the *barre*. The *barre* should be the right height so that you can go all the way down without raising your shoulder.

1. Stand sideways to the *barre*, feet in third, arm in second. Keep your arm, head, and legs moving smoothly together as you *plié*.

2. *Demi-plié* Keep shoulders and hips facing forward. Heels are always on the ground in *demi-plié*.

3. *Grand plié* Your arm is in *bras bas* as you reach *grand plié*—it comes up through first and opens to second as you come up.

Battements tendus

Battement means "beat," *tendu* means "to stretch." This exercise will make your legs, feet, and toes strong and prepare them for jumps and *relevés*. You will practice *battements tendus* in different directions and do several repetitions in each position. Your toes stay touching the floor as you slide out and in.

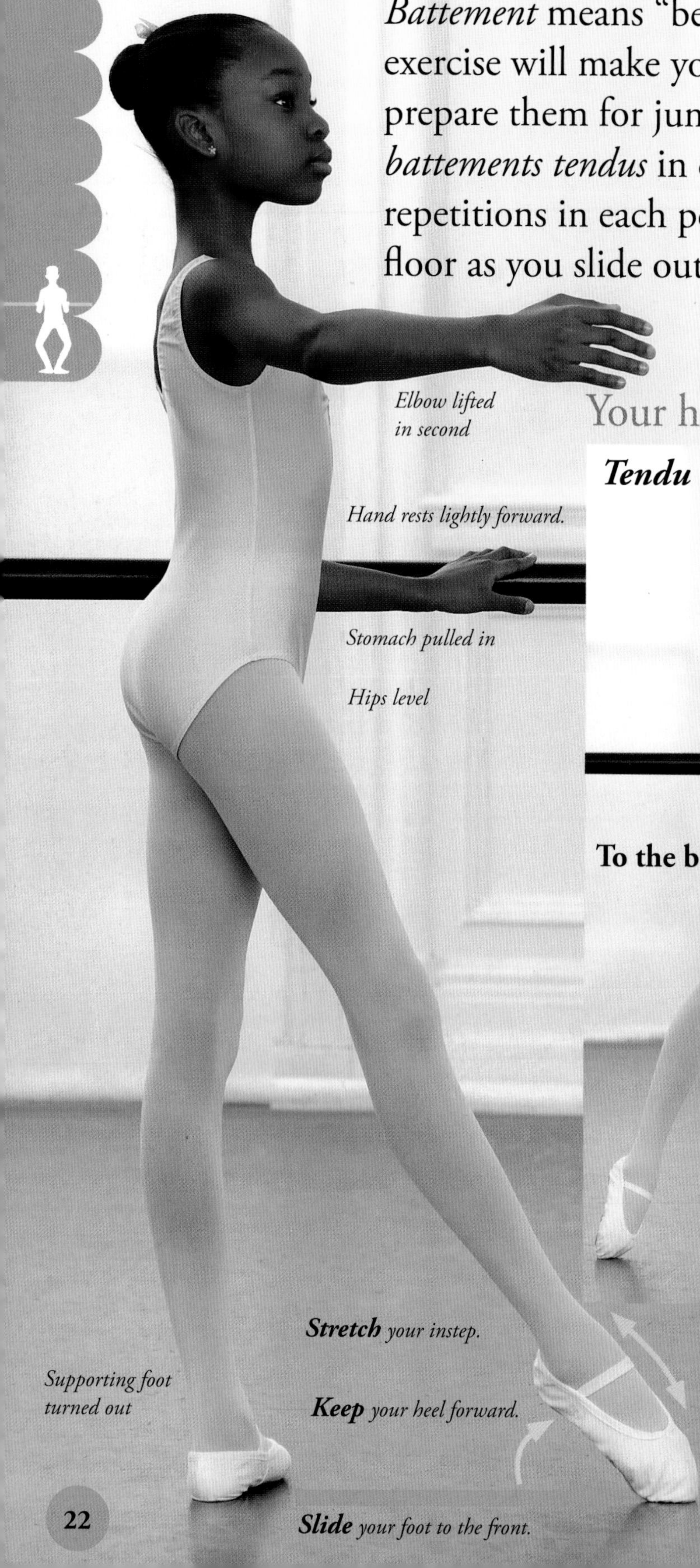

Elbow lifted in second

Hand rests lightly forward.

Stomach pulled in

Hips level

Your hand on the *barre* must stay in front

Tendu

To the back

To the side

Stretch *your instep.*

Supporting foot turned out

Keep *your heel forward.*

Slide *your foot to the front.*

Derrière (behind): Your body will have to lean slightly forward as you slide your foot behind. Turn your leg out from your hip and stretch behind your knee.

De côté (to the side): Keep your hips level and heel forward as you stretch your leg to the side, slightly in front of your hip.

Learning *tendus*

You can do a *tendu devant*, *de côté*, or *derrière* facing the *barre*. Keep your back straight as Hannah shows here, with your hands lightly resting forward on the *barre* and start from first position. As it becomes easier, you can start your *tendus* from third position. Remember to keep your legs turned out from the hips.

Relevé in French means *"to raise."*

Tendus stretch right down to the tip of your toes, lightly touching the floor.

of your body.

To the front

En croix

Most *barre* exercises are done *en croix* (in the shape of a cross). This means the movement is done to the front, the side, the back, and the side again. By doing the same move in different directions, you will use different muscles.

Joe's knees are pulled up, not back.

Derrière

De côté

Devant

Devant (front): Your heel leads the way as you stretch the leg forward, finishing in a beautiful, pointed foot. As Beverley shows, you should stand tall as you slide your foot out and in.

In a *tendu*, your foot never leaves the floor.

Battements glissé and grands battements

Glissé means "glide" and *grand* means "big." It's the same movement but the height of your leg is different. In *battement glissé*, you lift your toe a few inches off the ground. In *grand battement*, you swing your leg as high as it can go without letting your knee bend or spoil the position of your body.

Shoulders and hips face the front

Swing leg to hip level or higher and hold straight, as Beverley does here.

Grand battement devant

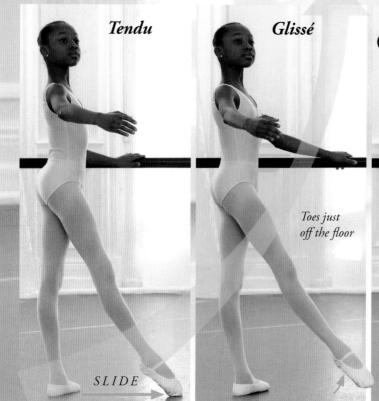

Tendu

Glissé

Toes just off the floor

SLIDE

1. Lift your upper body and press your feet into the floor as you slide through a **tendu devant**.

2. Continue the movement, swish your toes off the ground into a **glissé**...

3. ... and lift to the full height of your **grand battement**. As you lower the leg, return through the **glissé** and **tendu** position to close in third.

Learning *glissé* and *grand battement*

Start in first position facing the *barre* and slide your foot just off the ground to the *glissé* position as Hannah demonstrates here. Practice this several times to the front, side, and back, first with one foot and then the other. When this becomes easier, try swishing your leg a little higher with more energy to make a *grand battement*.

Slide

Grand battement *derrière*

Straight leg and pointed foot

You will have to lean slightly forward to lift your leg behind.

Joe slide's his hand forward on the barre as he lifts his leg.

"It's more important to keep your body in a good position than to lift your leg high."

Keep your supporting knee straight.

3. ... and continue to lift to **grand battement**. Try to keep both shoulders forward and not twisted to one side.

Turn out your supporting foot.

Tendu

Glissé

1. Hips and shoulders face forward as your back leg extends to **tendu derrière**.

2. Push your supporting foot into the ground as the back leg lifts to **glissé**...

Développés

These slow, smooth movements are the preparation for *adage,* a sequence of beautiful positions and balances that you will do later in the class. *Développés* require muscle strength and control to lift the leg through *retiré* and stretch out. Practice will help you gain this.

Stand tall like Joe to make room for your développé.

Let your hand slide forward.

Attitude derrière

Retiré derrière

Développé devant

Développé devant and passes smoothly through *attitude devant* before fully unfolding and then closing back to third.

Développé a là seconde (to second)

Développé a là seconde (to second) also unfolds slowly and smoothly to the side. Try to move your arms and legs together in a continuous movement.

1. Your back foot draws a line up your leg to touch behind your knee.

A *développé* is a slow
unfolding of the leg.

Retiré devant

Draw the toes of your front
foot up the front of your leg
to rest just under the knee
of your supporting leg. This
is the position you will use
when you do *pirouettes*
(turns on the spot).

Développé derrière

*Stretch your
foot fully.*

*Retiré devant
rests in front
of your knee.*

**Retiré
devant**

*Keep your
ankle and
foot strong for
good balance.*

2. Lift your knee and thigh
behind you to *attitude derrière*.

3. Unfold your leg behind you to *arabesque* and
stretch your arm forward. Keep your standing
leg straight. Lower and close to third position.

Relevés and rises

Relevé fifth

Ballet dancers should look very light on their feet, as if they can stay in the air or balance for a long time. Rises and *relevés* on to *demi-pointe* can help to give this impression. They are done in all five positions. *Relevé* means "raise" or "lift."

Similar steps

A rise and a *relevé* might look the same at first, but they are different movements. For a rise, your heels lift but your toes stay in the same place. For a *relevé*, give a little spring onto *demi-pointe* and move your toes underneath you.

Hands rest lightly for balance.

Do not lean on the barre.

Legs are turned out from the hips.

Relevé always starts from demi-plié.

Relevé means *"lift"* in French.

Relevé in fifth

Joe pulls his feet underneath him and his heels cross.

Legs are tightly closed.

Heels are forward.

Demi-pointe

When you are on *demi-pointe*, you are balanced on the balls of your feet. Push your feet down to the floor and lift your body away as you rise or *relevé*.

Feet are pulled toward each other in a relevé.

Sideways

As you get stronger you can stand sideways to the *barre* and use only one hand to help you balance. Feel a straight line from the floor to the top of your head.

Relevé derrière

Pirouette position

Relevé devant

Relevé in first

Joe pulls his feet underneath him and his heels touch.

Pirouette practice

Start from *demi-plié* in third position and spring onto *demi-pointe* with the raised leg in *retiré devant* as Beverley shows here. Take your hand off the *barre* and hold your balance. This is practice for a *pirouette* (a spin on *demi-pointe*).

Center practice

When you have finished your *barre* exercises, it's time to move into the middle of the room and try the positions and moves without the support of the *barre*. This is called center practice.

You will start with slow steps and *ports de bras* (arm exercises) and then do little jumps, traveling steps, combined steps, and finally bigger jumps using all the space in the room. Many dancers say that this is the part of the class that they like best.

WHAT THEY MEAN

en face *"face front"*
croisée *"crossed"*
effacé *"open"*
ouvert *"open"*
devant *"in front"*
derrière *"behind"*
à la seconde *"to second"*
en avant *"forward"*
en arrière *"backward"*

Croisée (crossed leg to the corner)

À *la seconde* (to the side)

Effacé (open leg to the corner)

Directions

Ballet steps can be done facing different directions. Imagine that you are standing in a square and each direction points to a different part of the square.

Croisée
"crossed"

En face
"face front"

Effacé
"open"

Croisée Face the corner of your square. Your audience will see your legs in a crossed position. Your shoulders and hips should also face toward the corner.

En face Face the front of your square, where your audience would sit. At first, you will learn most steps facing *en face*.

Effacé Face the corner of your square—your crossed leg should be away from the audience. Beverley is looking straight ahead— she could also look *en face*, to the audience.

TURNING STEPS

Facing different directions is preparation for turning steps. Nadja and Hannah are "spotting" as they spin around on *demi-pointe*. They keep looking at one spot while they turn; this stops them from feeling dizzy and helps them balance. As they turn, their bodies pass through all the directions in their imaginary squares.

1. Fix your eyes on a spot *en face* and keep looking at it as you start to turn.

2. Whip your head around to look at the same spot as you return to the front.

Traveling steps can move in different directions. The pattern that a dance makes when the steps travel around the room, or stage, is called the floor pattern.

En arrière

Moving backward is harder, especially if you are trying to follow a floor pattern. Remember to take your body weight back over your feet.

En avant

Traveling forward is the easiest direction because most of our everyday movements, such as walking or running, go forward.

En arrière "backward"

En avant "forward"

Adage

"*Adage*" means moving easily and smoothly. *Adage* will help you to get good balance and strong stomach and leg muscles as you move slowly and smoothly through each position. These are some of the best known positions in ballet.

Arabesque

One graceful *adage* involves moving the arms through three *arabesques*. Begin in first *arabesque*, with the same arm as leg stretched behind. Sweep your back arm around to the front, and your front arm to the back. Finally, move both in front for third *arabesque*.

First arabesque
The front arm is on the side of the standing leg.

Second arabesque
The front arm is on the side of the raised leg.

Third arabesque
Both arms forward, level with shoulder and eyeline

You can put together a sequence of graceful positions to make an *adage* exercise.

Tendu devant

Looking to the front of the room.

1. Start *tendu devant*, arms lifting to **demi-bras**. A correct starting position helps with the rest of the sequence.

Arabesque

Eyes looking out over the front hand.

Strong stomach for balance.

Supporting leg turned out.

2. Step (**posé**) forward, lift the leg and arms to first *arabesque*. The foot firmly placed on the ground will help you balance.

Foot firmly placed on floor.

Attitude

When you do *adage* exercises in class, you will often move through one or more of the *attitude* positions. Here, we show *attitude croisée derriére*, *attitude ouvert derriére*, and *attitude croisée devant*. Remember to keep the knee of your working leg higher than the foot.

Beverley demonstrates an **Attitude croisée derriére**. Her standing leg is closest to the front of the room.

Attitude ouvert derriére: Beverley's lifted leg is closest to the front.

Attitude croisée devant: Beverley's leg is lifted forward, turned out, with her heel upward.

Move slowly and smoothly from shape to shape.

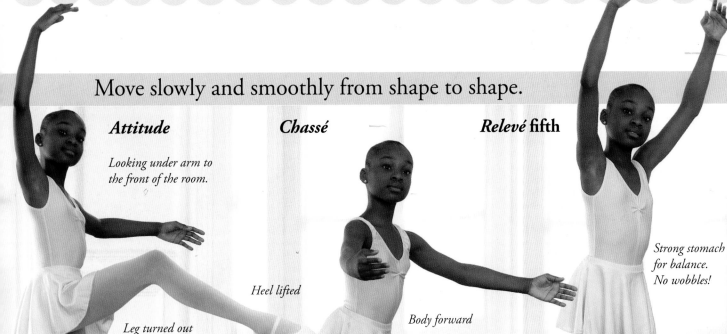

Attitude

Looking under arm to the front of the room.

Leg turned out from hip.

Chassé

Heel lifted

Body forward

Relevé fifth

Strong stomach for balance. No wobbles!

3. Lower your leg and pass through first position before lifting to *attitude devant*. Keep your leg turned out from the hip.

4. Take your body forward and place your foot down to a wide fourth position, front knee in soft **plié**—(bend).

5. **Relevé** onto **demi-pointe** as you close your feet tightly and lift your arms to fifth. Stay on balance, legs strong.

Petit allegro

Allegro steps are jumps—they are quicker and more lively than *adage*. First, you will do *petit allegro* (little jumps). If you have worked hard at your *pliés* and *tendus*, you will be able to do these light little jumps with beautifully stretched feet.

Lifted foot touches the calf

Petit jetés

These are little springs from foot to foot. Nadja and Hannah hold hands to practice *petit jeté derrière*. Their raised feet are pointed and touch the backs of their legs on the calf muscle.

Head moves from side to side.

Knees turned out as you lift and spring.

Calf muscle

Spring from foot to foot.

Sauté (jump) in first position

This is a simple jump so you can concentrate on stretching your legs and feet and landing in a neat first position each time. Remember, a good *demi-plié* is like a spring and will push you into the air.

Arms in first arabesque

Leg in arabesque

Posé en avant
(step forward)

Posé temps levé

Posé means "step"; *temps levé* is a hop on one foot. Nadja is doing a simple step forward and hop in first *arabesque*. Then she can swish the back foot forward and *posé temps levé* with the other leg and arm lifted. Try doing this while traveling in a circle around the room.

Foot stretches as it pushes from the ground.

37

Traveling steps

It's fun to gallop or skip around the dance studio or across the stage. These steps can travel, or move, forward, sideways, or in a circle. Keep your head and arms in the correct position as you jump high and travel along. There is lots to remember!

Hold your head high and your back straight.

Lift your knee high on each skip.

Skips

Skips are light, high, and bouncy. Try to stretch your feet and point your toes as you skip high into the air. Remember to point the toes on your bottom foot, too!

LIKE A CAT

This step is called *pas de chat*, which means "cat step." To perform a good *pas de chat*, you must spring quickly into the air and land lightly on the floor. Cats move almost without a sound—try to land as quietly as you can.

Look where you're going.

Elbows lifted.

Knees turned out.

Back foot lifts first.

Weight on both feet.

1 Start in third position with *demi-plié*. In **pas de chat**, you travel towards the back foot and it's always the back foot that lifts first.

GALLOPS

At first, practice gallops keeping the same foot in front. Then try doing two gallops with the right foot in front and two with the left. Keep changing as you travel around the room.

1 Swish your front foot out and bend the other knee, ready to jump up.

2 Bring your back leg behind your front leg as you jump in the air and stretch your feet and knees.

3 As you come down from the jump, stretch the front leg forward, ready for the next gallop.

Try to keep your hands relaxed.

Your neck should be long and your head held high.

Keep your toes pointed downward as you leave the floor.

Keep looking in the direction you are traveling.

Bring your feet together neatly in the air. This might take some practice, but it will be well worth all the effort!

Retiré derrière

Push from the floor.

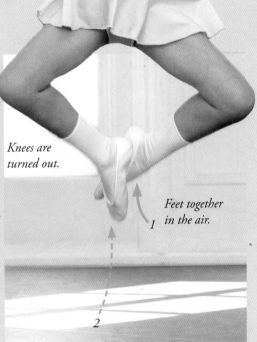

Knees are turned out.

Feet together in the air.

1

2

Front foot quickly closes to third position.

2

1

2 As you push up from the floor, lift your leg into a *retiré derrière*. Keep the movement smooth, and your arms softly in position.

3 As you spring in the air, quickly bring your front foot to meet your back foot. This will only be for a moment before the back foot starts to return to the floor.

4 Back foot lands before front foot quickly closes into third. Remember to start and finish in a *demi-plié*.

Allegro

Now try some bigger jumps. These are done with an easy bounce like a ball—we call this *ballon*. You must *plié* between each jump and make good positions in the air.

Soubresaut

Joe keeps his body in a straight line when he is in the air and pulls his legs and feet tightly together. This jump is especially good for boys to practice because later it will be done with a turn in the air, *tour en l'air*.

Knees stretched

Feet together and stretched

1. Demi-plié with legs turned out, ready to push into the air, arms in **bras bas**.

2. Bring your feet quickly together as you jump—it will look as if you have just one foot.

3. Land back on the same place that you jumped from, with the same foot in front.

40

Arms in arabesque

Shoulders and neck relaxed

Body weight forward to help you move forward.

Sissonne ouvert en avant

In this step, the legs open wide in the air, like a pair if scissors. You can do *sissonnes* in a variety of positions and different directions; this one starts with two feet on the ground, but lands on one leg.

Soft arms

Strong thighs

1. *Demi-plié* in a turned-out position, arms **bras bas**.

2. Shoot your legs away from each other as you jump forward into **arabesque**.

3. Land on one leg in *demi-plié*, keeping your back straight. This will strengthen your thigh muscles.

Music will help you to jump. Remember to breathe deeply.

1. Beverley is in a turned-out *demi-plie* position to prepare for the jump.

2. Beverley jumps straight up with her feet together, before changing her front foot.

3. Beverley lands softly in a deep *demi-plié* with the other foot in front.

Changement

This jump goes straight up and down, like a *soubresaut*, but your front foot changes to the back when you are in the air. Practicing a sequence of these will help you get a stronger jump. Remember to change your foot position on each jump.

Feet in fifth position.

Land with the other foot in front.

Grand allegro

Grand allegro means big, lively jumping steps. Remember all the things you have learned: positions, turnout, *ports de bras*, steps, directions, traveling, *ballon*. You will need them all to jump high and move fast.

Enchaînement

An *enchaînement* (chain) is a sequence of steps danced one after another. Now that you have learned several different *allegro* steps, try putting them together in an *enchaînment*. Each step should move smoothly into the next.

Grand allegro is the most exciting part of the class!

Allegro enchaînement

1. Sissonne en avant   2. Chassé (slide) en avant   3. Pas de chat

GRANDS JETÉS

Jeté means "to throw" and there are many different ways to do a *jeté*. You have already read about *petits jetés*—this is a *grand* (big) *jeté*. You will learn this step when you are older, after you have been doing *allegro* for some time. Practicing *grands battements* will make this step easier.

Echappé to second

4. Échappé à la seconde

5. Soubresaut

43

Cool-down

The end of your practice or class should be calm, with slow moves and stretches. It's important to let your body cool down gradually, and for the muscles to relax.

Révérence

The class always finishes with a curtsey or bow—this is called a *réverénce*. It's a way of saying "thank you," and also good for cooling down. After a performance, dancers do a *réverénce* to thank the audience for watching them.

Gentle cool-down

After *allegro*, you will be hot and your heart will be beating fast. A simple *port de bras* exercise is a good way to allow your body to cool down and your heart to return to its normal rate. Stand in first and think about relaxing your shoulders and back as you do easy waves with your arms.

Stretching exercises

When your muscles are warm, they will stretch more easily. After class is a good time to practice stretching. You should never stretch too much, and it should never be painful. It's best to increase your flexibility by a tiny amount each time you stretch.

Joe keeps his legs straight as he bends forward to stretch his hamstrings—first one side, then the other.

Port de bras

Beverley and Joe are doing a *port de bras* to the side to cool down and stretch. After all their hard work in the class, they make sure their muscles are stretched and relaxed. This will leave their bodies ready for their next practice. Remember to stretch both sides evenly.

This will stretch your thigh muscle. Joe uses his arms to make sure he does not stretch too far.

Beverley stretches her hips and gently rotates her spine. She tries not to move her hips as her shoulders turn.

Nadja tries to keep her back and legs straight as she leans forward to stretch her hamstrings.

Hannah increases her turnout and hip stretch as she sits in the "frog" position with a straight back.

Next steps

Some children enjoy doing ballet so much that they decide to spend most of their time studying it in the hope that one day, when they are older, they might join a ballet company.

Being a professional ballet dancer is hard work, but it's a wonderful job to have. Each day you are doing the thing you love most—dancing. You have the excitement of being involved in creating ballets for the theater, and the thrill of performing them for an audience.

Joe dances in The Nutcracker *with English National Ballet.*

Ballet school

If you really enjoy ballet and want to learn more, you will need to practice nearly every day. It can be hard to fit this in with school, homework, and hobbies, so some children go to full-time ballet school, where they can do everything in one place.

Ballet class

Each day in ballet class, the teacher helps the children to practice exercises. The children work together and help each other. Most of them live at the school and only see their parents during school vacations. It can be hard to be far away from your family, but the children are happy dancing.

Classes

Children at ballet school study all the usual subjects, such as math and English, as well as learning ballet. In anatomy class, they learn how their muscles and joints move.

En pointe

It's the strong muscles in her legs, ankles, and feet that let Maddie dance **en pointe**. You must not try this until you are at least 12 years old and your teacher says your muscles are strong enough.

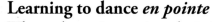

Learning to dance *en pointe*

When a dancer is *en pointe*, she is dancing on the tips of her toes. She wears special *pointe* shoes that have hard soles and toes to help support her feet. The shoes are kept in place with ribbons tied neatly around her ankles. When girls are learning *pointe* work, boys concentrate on jumps; there are one or two ballets where the men also dance *en pointe*.

Pas de deux

A *pas de deux* is a dance for two people. Learning to work with a partner is an important part of ballet training. When Maddie stands *en pointe* she can only balance for a few seconds. With Jesse's help she can stay on one leg and hold a beautiful *arabesque*. Partner work requires a lot of practice, especially if Maddie is wearing a tutu. This makes it harder for Jesse to hold her, but the dancers must make it look easy.

"You must trust your partner to hold you safely."

Fish dive

Arabesque

Jesse is strong enough to lift Maddie into a position called a fish dive. Both dancers have to concentrate on what they are doing to make sure that no one gets hurt.

Ready to perform

One of the nicest things is to show your dances to your family and friends. Perhaps your ballet school will have a performance in a theater and you will wear a costume and headdress.

COSTUMES

Costumes help to tell the story. A princess will wear a tutu with crystals and a tiara but Cinderella will have a simple dress, which looks old and torn. Costumes fit the character that the dancer is acting out.

Fix your tiara in place and it will sparkle under the lights.

Beautiful tutus

Maddie is wearing a tutu. This is a short dress, with a skirt made of stiff net that dancers wear. The first time that you wear a tutu is exciting, especially if it has beautiful decorations.

Boys wear tights and a shirt or tunic. Their costumes must not get in the way when they dance the big *allegro* steps or when they dance in a *pas de deux*.

BALLET BUN

1. A neat, high ponytail is made into a bun.

2. Twist the ponytail around and tuck the end under.

3. Fix it firmly in place with hairpins and a hairnet.

Performing on stage

Some ballets have parts for children to dance. Joe is excited because he has been chosen to dance in *The Nutcracker* with the English National Ballet.

Joe has a main role (part) as Freddie, sometimes called Fritz. He leads the children's dance in the party scene with Clara, his sister in the story.

Joe loves rehearsing and performing on stage with the older dancers because he hopes that one day he will also be a professional dancer.

Rehearsing

Maddie will rehearse her *pirouettes en pointe* many times before she dances on stage.

Ballet company

After ballet school, most young dancers hope to become professionals and join a ballet company. It takes a lot of hard work but, if you love to dance, it is the best job you could have.

Company class

Dancers in a company start each day with a ballet class to prepare their bodies. Then they spend the day rehearsing different ballets before putting on costumes and makeup to perform for an audience. There is usually a pianist to play music for class and rehearsals. Sometimes the dancers perform to music played by an orchestra.

> "Even professional dancers start each day with a class to perfect their steps."

BALLET NOTATION

The steps will be written down in a special way called a dance notation. Most ballet companies have a notator—someone trained to read the steps and help the dancers to learn them.

Making a ballet

The person who thinks of all the ideas and steps for a ballet is called a **choreographer**. Here, David Bintley is choreographing the Stars dance from *Cinderella*. He is one of the best-known choreographers in the world and has made ballets for many companies.

Rehearsal

Dancers have to rehearse for a long time before a ballet is ready to be performed on stage. Everyone must move together and dance in the same way. T he dancers who do the group dances are called the *corps de ballet*. This French name means "the body of the ballet."

Rehearsal for Swan Lake *performed by Royal Winnipeg Ballet, Canada.*

Stage makeup

Men and women wear makeup on stage. The colour and lines on the dancers eyes and mouths help the audience to see their faces clearly. Some roles need a special makeup to make the dancers look different.

"Performing in front of an audience makes all the hard work worthwhile."

Costumes

Different costumes are made for each ballet. They are often decorated with crystals and sequins to make them shine and sparkle. Dancers must rehearse in their costumes and headdresses before they perform on stage.

Alina Cojocaru as Cinderella in The Royal Ballet's production of Cinderella

The performance

Ballets are usually performed in a theater. Bright lights shine on the dancers as they dance on stage, watched by hundreds of people. At the end, everyone claps and cheers.

Ballet stories

While some ballets are just beautiful movements set to music, others tell stories. There are no words, but if you watch and listen, they are easy to understand. The costumes, scenery, dancers, and music all tell the story.

The Royal Ballet's Iohna Loots as Clara in The Nutcracker

The Nutcracker   Music by Peter Ilyich Tchaikovsky

It's Christmas, and young Clara is given a nutcracker doll (left). She dreams that it comes to life, turns into a prince, and leads the toy soldiers under the Christmas tree into battle against the rats (right). After Clara helps the Nutcracker Prince win the battle, she goes on a magical journey with him through the land of snow to the Kingdom of Sweets. Snowflakes, flowers, and candy canes dance for her, but most beautiful of all is the Sugar Plum Fairy.

Junor Souza as the Nutcracker Prince attacks James Streeter's Rat King.

Swan Lake   Music by Peter Ilyich Tchaikovsky

When Prince Siegfried goes to shoot a flock of swans, their queen, Odette, steps in (right). The swans are really girls, enchanted by the magician Rothbart. They will return to human form only if someone truly loves Odette. Siegfried pledges his love, but later he's tricked by Odile, Rothbart's daughter (far right), into thinking *she* is Odette, and he promises to love *her*. When he realizes the truth, he rushes to the lake to find Odette. Vowing to be together forever, they plunge into the water. The power of their love breaks Rothbart's spell.

Zinaida Yanowsky as Odette in The Royal Ballet production of Swan Lake.

When Cinderella's nasty stepmother and stepsisters go to the prince's ball, she's left alone in the cold house. A fairy godmother gives Cinderella a beautiful dress and a carriage so she can go to the ball, too, but warns her that she must be home by midnight, when the magic spell will be broken. Cinderella dances with the prince, but as the clock strikes 12, she runs away, leaving her shoe behind. The prince searches for the beautiful girl who fits the shoe. He finds Cinderella, and they are married.

The Royal Ballet production of Cinderella, *with Alina Cojocaru (left) in the title role, and Johan Kobborg (above) as the prince.*

Chi Cao as Prince Siegfried and Nao Sakuma as Odile.

Romeo and Juliet   Music by Serge Prokofiev

Danced by Tiits Heliments and Gaylene Summerfield, Romeo and Juliet die together in her tomb.

Romeo and Juliet fall in love, but their warring families do not allow them to be together. They secretly run away and get married (left). Juliet's parents try to force her to marry another man, so she drinks a potion that makes her fall into a deep sleep—everyone believes she's dead. Romeo also thinks this, and he kills himself in her tomb. When Juliet wakes from her deep sleep, she sees Romeo dead and kills herself (above).

Friar Lawrence (Jonathan Payn) marries Romeo (Iain Mackay) and Juliet (Jenna Roberts).

The Sleeping Beauty   Music by Peter Ilyich Tchaikovsky

Carabosse (Deirdre Chapman) issues a curse at Aurora's christening in The Royal Ballet's The Sleeping Beauty.

Natasha Oughtred as Aurora pricks her finger at her 16th birthday party.

Fairies bring gifts to the christening of Princess Aurora. Carabosse, a wicked fairy, is angry that she wasn't invited, and mimes a curse that Aurora will prick her finger and die when she is older. The Lilac fairy mimes that she will not die, but sleep for a hundred years. On Aurora's 16th birthday, she pricks her finger (right) and everyone at the court falls asleep. Eventually, a prince out hunting finds Aurora and wakes her with a kiss. They fall in love. At their wedding, fairy-tale characters come to dance.

The Dream — Music by Felix Mendelssohn

The Dream is based on Shakespeare's play *A Midsummer Night's Dream*

Matthew Lawrence is Oberon (left and right), while Nao Sakuma is Titania (right).

The fairy king, Oberon (left), and queen, Titania (above center) are quarreling. Oberon's servant, Puck, creates confusion with his mischievious magic—various lovers argue and Titania falls in love with a man (Bottom) wearing a donkey's head (below left). In the end, all is put right, Titania and Oberon are friends, and the lovers are happily united. The male dancer playing the part of Bottom dances *en pointe*—his shoes are the donkey's hooves.

As bottom, James Grundy dances en pointe.

Coppélia — Music by Léo Delibes

Swanilda (Rachael Peppin) and Franz (Tiits Heliments) in the pas de deux.

A young man (Franz) is fascinated by the old toymaker Dr. Coppélius and the life-sized doll in his window (Coppélia) (left). Franz's girlfriend (Swanhilda) is jealous—she and her friends creep into Dr. Coppélius' workshop and pretend to be his dolls. Dr. Coppélius believes he has succeeded in bringing the dolls to life until he realizes that he's been tricked. Later, when Franz and Swanhilda marry, the whole village celebrates, and Dr. Coppélius is invited to the party.

Swanilda (Elisha Willis) pretends to be Coppélia to fool Dr. Coppélius (Michael O'Hare).

Famous feet

Ballet dancers are famous and loved for many reasons—
some display incredible technique, some have extraordinary
strength, and some are great interpreters of dance drama.
A few even move beyond the world of ballet to become
popular celebrities as well as legendary dancers.

*Margot Fonteyn and Rudolph Nureyev in
The Royal Ballet's Romeo and Juliet*

The Royal Ballet's Cinderella, *with
Antoinette Sibley and Anthony Dowell*

The Nutcracker, *Kirkland and Baryshnikov,
American Ballet Theatre staging*

Margot Fonteyn
(1919–1991)

British ballerina Dame Margot Fonteyn
was an early member of the Vic-Wells Ballet
(later The Royal Ballet), creating many roles
with choreographer Frederick Ashton.
During her sparkling 40-year career, she
had many partnerships, but her most
famous was formed with Rudolph Nureyev,
when she was 43, and he was only 22.

Rudolf Nureyev
(1938–1993)

Trained at the Kirov in Russia, Nureyev
is famous for his astonishing technique
and dramatic performances, as well as
his partnership with Margot Fonteyn.
Nureyev was not only a gifted dancer,
but he was also an internationally famous
figure who revived popular interest in
ballet during the 1960s.

Antoinette Sibley
(1939–)

Considered the ideal British ballerina,
Antoinette Sibley joined The Royal Ballet
in 1956, becoming a soloist in 1960. She
and her partner Anthony Dowell created
many roles, including Titania and
Oberon in *The Dream,* and they appeared
in all the leading classical ballets such as
Swan Lake and *The Nutcracker.*

Anthony Dowell
(1943–)

Like Antoinette Sibley, Dowell trained at
The Royal Ballet School, and joined the
company in 1961. He had a long and
successful career as a principal dancer,
admired for his precise technique and
restrained English style. Later, he became
Artistic Director of The Royal Ballet, a
position he held from 1986 until 2001.

Mikhail Baryshnikov
(1948–)

Also trained at the Kirov, Baryshnikov
danced with both New York City
Ballet and American Ballet Theatre (often
with Gelsey Kirkland) between 1974
and 1979, and displayed his virtuoso
technique with other companies around
the world. Later, he became Artistic
Director of American Ballet Theatre.

Gelsey Kirkland (1952–)

Trained at the School of American
Ballet, Kirkland joined New York City
Ballet in 1968, at age 15. A great dramatic
ballerina, she created a number of roles
there for choreographer George
Balanchine. In 1974, she joined American
Ballet Theatre, and later performed as a
guest artist with The Royal Ballet.

Viviana Durante and Irek Mukhamedov in Manon *with The Royal Ballet*

Irek Mukhamedov
(1960–)

Mukhamedov began his career with the Bolshoi Ballet in Moscow, where he was the youngest-ever dancer to perform the role of *Spartacus*. In 1990, he joined The Royal Ballet, where he danced with Darcey Bussell. Now retired, Mukhamedov had a strong, muscly body, and was known as one of the world's greatest dramatic dancers.

Viviana Durante
(1967–)

Born in Rome, Viviana Durante trained mainly at The Royal Ballet School. She joined the company in 1983 and became a principal at the age of 21. During her time at The Royal Ballet, she performed many classical and modern roles and gained an international reputation as both a technically strong and a dramatic ballerina. In 1999, she joined American Ballet Theatre, and went on to perform as guest artist all over the world, appearing at La Scala, Milan, and with The Royal Ballet and the Tokyo Ballet. In 2010, she founded the Viviana Durante Comany in the UK.

Wendy Whelan
(1967–)

A principal dancer with New York City Ballet, Wendy Whelan trained at the company's School of American Ballet. Her flexibility and athleticism are perfectly suited to the ballets of George Balanchine, the company's founder, and she has appeared in many of his works, as well as classical ballets such as *The Nutcracker* and *Swan Lake*.

Wendy Whelan as the Sugar Plum Fairy in New York City Ballet's The Nutcracker

Darcey Bussell
(1969–)

A product of The Royal Ballet School and a principal dancer with The Royal Ballet, Bussell is considered one of the greatest of all English ballerinas. In 1989, she became the youngest-ever dancer to be promoted to principal, went on to perform many classical roles, including Odette/Odile in *Swan Lake*, the Sugar Plum Fairy in *The Nutcracker*, and Aurora in *The Sleeping Beauty*, and appeared in a wide range of modern works. She has also performed as a guest artist with companies worldwide. In 2007, she retired from the company.

Darcey Bussell in The Royal Ballet's production of Winter Dreams

Julie Kent
(1969–)

A principal with American Ballet Theatre since 1993, Julie Kent has performed a large range of classical and modern ballets in her career. She has also won several international ballet prizes, including the Erik Bruhn Prize.

Carlos Acosta
(1973–)

Born one of 11 children in Cuba, Acosta studied ballet as a way out of the family's poverty. By the time he was 20, he was dancing with the world's leading companies, and most regularly with The Royal Ballet. In addition to major classical roles, Acosta performs many modern works, and in 2007 he became the first western dancer to perform the role of *Spartacus* with the Bolshoi Ballet.

Carlos Acosta in The Royal Ballet's Rhapsody

Julie Kent as Juliet, with Vladimir Malakov as Romeo at the Deutsche Oper, Berlin

"I try to bring **SOMETHING** for **everybody**."

Johan Kobborg
(1972–)

Born in Denmark and trained at the Royal Danish Ballet School, Kobborg joined The Royal Ballet in 1999, and since then he has danced most of the leading classical roles, including the prince in *The Nutcracker* and *Cinderella*, Siegfried in *Swan Lake*, Romeo, and Albrecht in *Giselle*. He is frequently cast alongside Romanian dancer Alina Cojocaru, who is also his offstage partner. Together, they have appeared together in *Giselle* with the Kirov Ballet.

Alina Cojocaru
(1981–)

Born in Bucharest, Romania, Cojocaru had her early training in Romania, then at the Kiev Ballet school in the Ukraine. In 1997, at age 16, she won the gold medal at the Prix de Lausanne International ballet competition, plus a six-month scholarship to train at The Royal Ballet School in London. Eventually, she joined the company and was made principal in 2001. Since then, she and Johann Kobborg have formed a strong partnership in a wide range of classical and modern roles.

Johann Kobborg and Alina Cojocaru in The Royal Ballet staging of The Sleeping Beauty.

Roberto Bolle
(1975–)

Born in Italy, Roberto Bolle trained at the La Scala Theatre Ballet School and was later a principal at La Scala, Milan. At 21, he left to pursue a freelance career and has since performed with companies all over the world, including the Tokyo Ballet, the Stuttgart Ballet, the National Ballet of Canada, the Royal Ballet, and American Ballet Theatre in New York. He is a Goodwill Ambassador for UNICEF.

Roberto Bolle, In the Middle, Somewhat Elevated, The Royal Ballet

Ivan Vasiliev
(1989–)

Stocky and powerful, Ivan Vasiliev has often been compared to both Rudolph Nureyev and Mikhail Baryshnikov. Born in Vladivostok, Russia, he is a principal at the Bolshoi Ballet, where his incredible jump is shown off in *Spartacus*, *Don Quixote*, *La Bayadere*, and *Le Corsaire*. He has also danced the part of Colas in Frederick Ashton's *La fille mal gardée*, also with the Bolshoi Ballet.

Ivan Vasiliev in the Bolshoi Ballet's Don Quixote

Natalia Osipova
(1986–)

Born in Moscow, Russia, Osipova pursued an early career as a gymnast before training as a ballet dancer. She went on to become a principal with the Bolshoi Ballet, where her extraordinary energy and technique were displayed in a wide variety of roles, from Kitri in *Don Quixote* to *Giselle* and Jeanne in *The Flames of Paris*. Osipova also performs regularly as guest artist with American Ballet Theatre.

Natalia Osipova as Swanilda in the Bolshoi Ballet's production of Coppélia.

Glossary

adage Slow, controlled movements performed to slow music.

allegro Quick, lively movements. This name is given to jumped ballet steps.

arabesque A position where one leg is straight, and extended behind the body. The name is taken from a graceful Moorish motif.

assemblé To assemble or bring together. A step in which the legs are brought together in the air.

à terre On the ground.

attitude A position with rounded arms and a bent raised leg.

balancé A waltz step.

ballerina The highest rank of female dancer in a company.

ballon Bounce. This term describes the light, springy feeling a dancer should bring to small jumps and movements on the ground.

barre A long horizontal handrail that dancers use for support when practicing.

battement Beating. A straight, strong action of the leg used in many exercises and steps.

bras bas Arms low. A low, round position of the arms used for finishing movements or resting.

changement Change. A small jump in which the feet change position in fifth (or third) position.

chassé To chase. A small, sliding step in which one foot "chases" the other.

choreography Putting steps together to make a dance.

coordination Moving different body parts at the same time.

cou-de-pied Neck of the foot. "*Sur le cou-de-pied*" is a position in which one foot wraps around the other ankle.

coupé To cut. A move where one foot takes the place of the other.

croisée Crossed. A position where the body is slightly turned, and the audience sees the legs crossed.

curtsy See *révérence.*

de côté To the side.

demi-bras Half arms. A position where arms are halfway between first and second positions, with hands facing out.

demi-plié Half bend. A small bend with the feet flat on the floor.

demi-pointe Half *pointe.* A position where you stand on the balls of the feet, halfway between flat and full *pointe.*

demi-seconde Half second. A position where arms are held lower than second position, as if resting on a tutu.

derrière Behind.

devant In front.

développé To unfold. A smooth, unfolding movement of the leg.

downstage The area between the center of the stage and the front edge.

échappé To escape. A movement where the legs spring open at the same time.

en arrière Moving backward.

en avant Moving forward.

enchaînement A chain. A sequence of linked steps.

en croix In the shape of a cross. A sequence of moves that go to the front, the side, and the back.

en dedans When the leg moves in a circle, going toward the body.

en dehors When leg moves in a circle, going away from the body.

en diagonale On a diagonal.

en face Facing the front.

en l'air In the air.

en manège Originally a circus ring. A series of steps performed in a circle.

en pointe Dancing on the tips of your toes in special blocked (stiffened) shoes.

gallop A traveling step where you bring your feet together in the air.

glissé Gliding. A *battement glissé* (gliding *battement*) is a *battement tendu* that's lifted a little way off the floor.

grand battement Big beat. A *battement glissé* that's lifted high into the air.

grand jeté Big throw. A high jump in which the weight is transferred from one leg to the other.

grand plié Big bend. A full bend of the knees with the body upright.

instep The arch in the middle of your foot.

jeté To throw. A jumping step that starts with one leg "thrown" out, and lands on the other leg. (*See grand jeté*)

ouvert Open. A position where the body is slightly turned, and the legs are not crossed.

pas de bourrée A step named after a French dance (*bourrée*) that has quick, small steps.

pas de chat Cat step. A light jump with the feet taking off and landing one after the other.

pas de deux Step for two. A dance for two people.

petit allegro Small, quick jumps.

petit jeté Little throw. A springing step from foot to foot.

piqué To pick up. A step in which the foot is lifted quickly.

pirouette To whirl. A turn on one leg, where the working foot is lifted to the knee of the supporting leg.

plié A bend of the knees. (*See also demi-plié, grand plié*)

port de bras Carriage of the arms. A sequence of arm positions.

posé A step onto one foot, *demi-pointe,* or full *pointe.*

posture The way you stand.

relevé To raise. A quick movement onto *demi-pointe* or *pointe.*

retiré To draw away. A position where one raised foot touches the other knee.

révérence A smooth movement where the knees bend and the head lowers. Sometimes called a curtsy, a *révérence* expresses thanks, and is often done at the end of a ballet class or performance.

rise A lifting of the heels.

soubresaut A jump in which the legs are held tightly together in the air.

spotting The technique of whipping your head around and focusing your eyes on one spot as you turn. This stops you from getting dizzy.

sur place In the same place.

temps levé Lifted count. A hop.

temps lié Linked count. A step in which one leg moves, then the other, with a transfer of weight.

tendu To stretch. Usually, one leg in a stretched position.

turnout The basic position of the legs in ballet—turned out from the hip joints to the feet.

tutu A ballet dress with a skirt made of layers of net.

upstage The area of space between the center of the stage and the back.

wings The row of narrow curtains or flats that hang at the side of the stage. Dancers usually arrive and leave the stage from the wings.

Index

Acknowledgments

DK would like to thank... **FREED** OF LONDON for supplying dancewear (www.freedoflondon.com). **Dancers:** Joseph Sissens, Beverley Adeboye, Nadja and Rowan Shone, Hannah Rosenheim, Madeleine Shimwell, and Jesse Milligan. **Locations:** TringPark Tring Park School for the Performing Arts for kind permission to feature their premises and students (www.tringpark.com). We would also like to thank The Urdang Academy for providing locations. **Photographic assistance:** Carly Churchill. **Picture research:** Rob Nunn. **Design assistance:** Gemma Fletcher, Rosie Levine, Lauren Rosier, and Mary Sandberg.

Picture credits

The publisher would like to thank the following for their kind permission to reproduce their photographs:
(Key: a-above; b-below/bottom; c-center; l-left; r-right; t-top)
Bill Cooper / BC Arts Photography: 46-47, 51bl, 51cl, 52crb, 53bl, 54cra, 54tl, 54-55b, 55br, 55tl, 55tr, 56br, 56tl, 56tr, 57bl, 57cl, 57crb, 57tl, 57tr, 59c, 60b, 60tr, 61l. Corbis: Bettmann 58cr; Robbie Jack 61br; Douglas Kirkland 53crb; Barry Lewis 48cra; Paul A. Souders 53tl. Getty Images: Echo 48crb. Reuters: Fabrizio Bensch 60cla. Rex Features: ITV 58cl; Reg Wilson 58c, 59tl. TopFoto. co.uk: Nigel Norrington / ArenaPAL 61tr; Johan Persson / ArenaPAL 52cla, 53ca, 56cl; Linda Rich / ArenaPAL 59tr. All other images © Dorling Kindersley
For further information see: www.dkimages.com